The Mercury Road

The Mercury Road

poems by

Mac Oliver

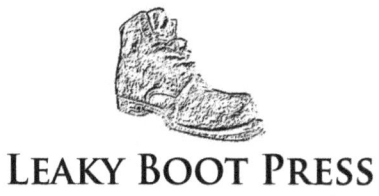

LEAKY BOOT PRESS

The Mercury Road
by Mac Oliver

First published in 2016 by
Leaky Boot Press
http://www.leakyboot.com

ISBN: 978-1-909849-35-8

To Albino Carrillo and Robert Stark

"radioactive, pal?"

Contents

Section I

Section II

Section I

Arid, Twilit

My fellow traveler, a city out of Bunyan
Beckons, pulls us in: a year-round fair
That seems a new erection but it's old,
The oldest town of all, an auctioneer
Of lands, elections, pearls & bodies, red
At dusk as any battlefield
Before debris gets cleared, where lean
And flashy guides lead street to street a tour
Across the kingdom of allurements, tricks,
A debtor's prison we'd be wise to stay
Away from, as from watchmen, cops.

I've had too long to think aesthetics,
Dream I'm stuck again, again, like I'm
Some mastodon in tar that looks like water
Under cover of the night, my limbs
Already sunk. I'm cognizant I'm down,
My gullet last to clog before I cough
The glue lodged in its opening. I feel
Again an arid, twilit thirst.
The outskirts of the town are howling,
Like all of it does not exist: Farewell.

Coyote hunting at the crossroads
Of the drunkard's walk…
Can't coax a tainted sky for rain,
For aspergation…

Bishop's ring diffracting alpenglow,
The rising roar of engines through the haze
Of aerosols, above the chromium,
Can you recall a day before this night?

As If

Our Lady of the Road, beneath my feet,
We scout a half a century ahead,
The hand that holds
The pen already cold, no doubt our fate
Is different but in the thirst's degree.
The leaky faucet kills, the fertile valleys
Carthaginian with salt, as if
The grave centurions threw rocks of it
In every furrow, underneath the water
Cornered, district drained, no snow to fill
The reservoir, its bed a wreath of dust,
The till to fill a fault.

Desert Jams

Next over in the seat a collared shade,
The poet left beside himself, will strike
The dash impatiently, at intervals,
And cry, free as the road, loose as the wind,
I will not be tied up in desert jams,
No rope of sand will noose this neck, lasso
This open throat, no lariat's going
To hang me high. I am a disciplined
Cadaver now, a mendicant who seeds
The singing mustard down the Mission Road,
A guide to wanderers, these sunburnt hills,
Their radiance, their lore discernable;
My hymnal made of the horizon line,
A witness to the human want of love.

Windstorms, dust tongues through safety glass,
Distortions of the sun through shifting sands:
The desert sky becomes a tiger's face,
All streaks of furnace, foaming mouth,
Words reduced to something like a thirst
You can't remember how to satisfy,
But must, the meantime moaning driest sighs
Across the desert road, the gasoline
Beneath the hood in flames, the grill a set
Of teeth to hide the fanning blades that cool
The firing engine's rev.

Streaking Luck

Las Vegas: up it goes in emerald
Like Oz, its towers beckoning, the nude
Beside the praying saint: Come satisfy
Your thirst, she says, but wear these first, these shades
Of green, these special glasses, set the glow
Upon your nose: you'll get to meet the wizard.
Easy, vulgar trifling with awe…
Here fakes take on incantatory power,
Oratorical mendacity,
Deft tongues, the barker, charlatan, the witty
Demonstration of a vanished coin.
I've seen the booty tabulated, heard
The bitter bettors curse their streaking luck,
And swear on deities of watered sand.

Off the Dash

Hail, Citizens of Ooze, lubricious sheets
Of gaudery, the dunce & entourage,
This "insubstantial pageant", stagy boasts.
Lake Mead or Lake Stymphalia?
The birds of Ares (Nellis), claws of brass,
The distant light of Alpha Lyrae, beta
Burns across your naked thyroid, gamma
Rays, your throat a blasted reed, can find
No comforter, but like old Bottom sing
To keep the monsters flickering at the edge.

A fleet of gamblers hurried up to wait,
And held us back beneath the Martial sun,
The dust of August, solar radiation
Flashing off the dash. The lizards did
What looked like pushups, braced against the dunes.
Re-circulating air-conditioning
Was sickening us after a while, impossible:
Hallucinations came unlimited,
Religions lost, sects since died out,
Who watered sand with sobs
And futile oaths, laments, no manna…

EXPECT DELAYS

A Fragile Band

You strike a match: it is a notable
Explosion, flash of sulphur… now imagine,
Ignominious, beyond all war,
But twice. The argument of arms? Set off
Defeat is total, finalizing, leveling
Foolishness, that farce of rival force,
Deterrence still intact, a fragile band
Of treaties, never cooled, a venom fresh
As summer dawn, no antidote at all:
The guilt upon my head. How could I let
A yawp lie idle in this cause, not seize
Resources coursing through your memory,
The rest be damned. I wouldn't harness Pluto.
No, I plot against his ministers,
Ignatius of insomniacs,
My book a list of birds,
My coracle a drifting bark,
My oracle a calumet of leaves,
The sniff of oranges, a handful, grass,
A skunk, a loaf of rye, unfiltered juice
Of passion fruit & sugar cane,
Eat chocolate, eat avocado,
Quaff piping Joe, these foods the bard's
New World grub. I see how Pluto's is
The longest reign of all. A bargain
Ill-advised… severe plutonium.

Mountain War Time

5:29am,
Mountain War Time,
July 16th 1945:
"It works… it works."

First heat, dilated sight, exploding
Sudden splendor, atoms scattered, heavy
Change: what stem & cap of spores
Is cankering the rosy sky? By tents,
On lawn chairs lounged as if to tan, their fore-
Heads lifted, bathed in balls of light, their jaws
Hinged low in awe, or tightly grinding teeth
Beneath thin, lipless smiles, Generals
See stars. The faculty who tinkered crane,
Victorious as Pyrrhus: proud conversion,
Precious raw to cooked & ready
Weaponry, the race's winners, retinas
Scarred with a high sort of seeing, can't be sure
This power suits their slumping shoulders well.

"It works & is."

Heavens Opening?

A few look back & linger there with dread:
Which shawl is this enfolding us in arms?
What power tested, waking forth?
A fire's fuel of air, ravine
Of radiation, cosmic blotches,
Blains, malignancies downwind,
Worse ills to come…

The human being burns with this: a hare-
Brained episode without a written end.
With such a burden one goes down, unfit
To bear it. Generations listen for
A messenger, the voice of one who cries
Vociferously, a mouth: will you come,
Heavens opening? Two mourning doves
Fly through the dawn. A flash of light breaks forth,
The sun is muscular, the concept rains
On darkling witnesses: what has man wrought?
You dream, had I been there… but what could I
Have done? The future won't forget this past,
What it produced won't drop away, though wind
Without regard the rest destroys.

I'm on my knees guts twisted, breath runs out,
With organ pain. I wish to neutralize
The danger zones, clear out the magazines,
The fallout solved somehow, the gamble won,
No meteor to crash the arsenal,

But gutsy harp to keep at bay the ferryman
Whose limbs are juniper & shaggy pine.

Boulders, stones rebounding into dust, it sounds!
Blast radius too wide, hard thermal pulse,
Thrashed by drizzling hail.

Shock Wave

I've felt that evil too, a fever, let
The lever fly, my ego die to find
You right, the Theological Moment, words
I can't improve, already happened. Fall
Asleep? That's only natural, as even
For an hour Peter couldn't keep
Awake, denies his Lord & cries, to whom
Christ said, Sleep now & take your rest.
It is enough. The hour's come:
He was betrayed.
The shock wave took less than a minute
Like an oven door left open, said a few.
Now East & West on all flat maps are one.

Now East & West on all flat maps have folded
Into one, the globe reduced in size
To tiny—Trinity, the coup de grâce...
Nearby—Socorro, our Señora del Socorro—
Conquistadors were given corn & water
In the village called Teypana, half-
Dead from vicious thirst for gold along
The Rio Grande, Jornada del Muerto.
Tectonically it is a rift. The lithosphere
Once stretched like taffy, left alluvium
In beds... The half-life of Plutonium
Is twenty four thousand years.
This clap's a mighty trumpet.
No more about the golden atoms...

What Can Be Fit

The future has betrayed
Its darker purposes. It isn't far
From here to where they tested atom bombs.
The rust is on the plant that made the fuel.
What can be fit against this lasting fall?
Strong rocky caves? The whole thing starts again.
We grow into the dark. The mockingbird
Is unaware what threat has now arisen near
His thriving song along the barbed wire fence
Before the crack of dawn. The lizards spawn
Beside the crawling line of idling cars.

The atom splitting, ceaseless roar is faint
For now, that wind of fire robbing bones
Of flesh, that leveling off of all
That cuts down great & small to dusty dunes
That shift & sift as soft & swift as time
In glass & smooth millennia...

Motor Phlegm

The desert, bitter sea-less beach of glass
And salt where heat is blistering...
But for the air conditioning ghost towns
For now the boom goes on,
Behold the sprawling tract oases
Raised around a palm.
It's dry & far out here.
Heat tricks the eyes with sights
That aren't there, your throat on fire.
Delayed along the Spanish Trail! Oi.
I wouldn't conquer much, unarmed along
The Mormon Corridor,
The Hoover Dam Night Camp,
The crook who rolled with rocket fins
Well-oiled gangster, popped
At last gang-style, where ministers have flies
Unzipped for them, their simony pays off.

When suddenly the engine power seizes
Says I'm working hard, too hot,
I'm going to cough up motor phlegm
The air conditioning demands more juice
Than I can give it; were this horseback
You'd have buried me out here by now.

A pit stop at the shock wave's edge,
Through open desert, hurried, slowed.
This aqua Mercury runs grudgingly,
Its brake shoes feathered down to thinnest tin.

Life Athwart the Rivulets

How did I come to dwell on atom bombs?
A traffic jam on Sunday afternoon,
Our surge to California verging on
Conclusion when Las Vegas gamblers
Clogged the road, Nevada's outskirts
Through Los Angeles, the megalopolis
A centipede of stop & go, I thought
About the desert's growing thirst
Unsolvable, & all those rods of waste
Defy belief, & conjuring dire tricksters
Burlesque your grief. No turning back
To see the arid shade
Irradiated, salty, shattered hills,
But Orpheus can't help his backward glance,
Inheritance, felt gravely threatened, life
Athwart the rivulets: what'll thrive then?
How came we to this shore?
Can you recall a time before this shell?

Bill Still Out

The bargain was, in years, just twenty-four,
But what Faust gets is waste to last
A thousand generations, Mary & Joseph,
A gift not from Prometheus,
But Epimetheus, that match
Exploding, wish a mere cliché,
No myth, mere ricochet
Would blast the roots beneath the moss,
The flight of moths cut short,
Growth's conclusion, all abundance
Forfeited, no pansies freaked
With jet, nor dreams of freakish snows.

I hear the Neoterics of the Hanford Reach
Three generations down, the bill still out,
Contemplate bards of the spill, the tainted scales,
The sonneteers of rods once fuel, of tubes
Of eschatology, who prize the grinding gears,
Slowed down. I recollect some airborne stunts,
Salutes so flashy, lean, old awe in new
Technology we learned we paid for, zipped
Up flight suits, dashes through the clouds well-armed,
A trailing fluff left singed with orange tinge.

Stick Around

The Smiling Buddha detonates:
What trafficking in mockery is this?
What blessing in this blast? Can you recall
A time before this cell? O Soul, a Passage!
Do not leave me comfortless, life's light
Made viperous, our poverty, a snake
You won't expect, with fangs that overflow.
Can you recall a time before you felt
This threat, this woe, this great calamity?

Plutonium has split, but rods
Still thick with it will stick around.
The longest reign of all is Pluto's, Death:
That's hard enough.
Teach me to see the bigger light,
The globe in beams of heaven's fire,
Half sunk in mire.
Can you recall a time before this cell,
Our steps ashore?

Would Need The Muse

Can you recall a time before this shell?
From my first breath, asthmatic boy, this Earth
Was marred, this "Great Blue Marble" on
A pedestal, buoy on el mar.

Come froth & spray: the jetty stems the waves
The wind has capped with white, enshrouding shoals
Of feathery Achaean warriors, engaged
In argument of arms. The tide runs high
And red, gets civilized by spill of blood,
As once along Rhode Island shore I saw
The noxious crimson flood the Narragansett.
I'd provide the whole death list of tests,
As food for thought, this feat of detonation
Till for the lack of breath I'd need to puff
My atomizer, cloud of medicine,
You'd nod, you'd doze at such a bore
And dream of Oz, some pleasantry not here,
Somewhere the folks don't live in fear of fear.

We won't drive down the Mercury Road to see
The desert site, for all the radiation there:
The orders tapped to detonate, nine hundred
Tests beneath these sands. On go the names,
But I would need the muse that Homer called
Upon to catalogue the ships, to name
Them all, nor would you care to hear the list
In its entirety, or you would fall
Asleep like Mandelstam, your noggin down.

You'd dream of flight, the cranes like crowns enskied,
Half dozed, awake, your pillow calling back
Like a Confessor, cross a clouded screen,
This frequency in static lost, like sighs.
Can you remember sounds before this shell?

Beach Glass

Near Mercury spread parking lots where cars
Won't park, of Trinitite, a polar green,
As Tintoretto's painting, Peter over
Hull & tentatively toeing waves
Of Galilee, chopped up by gusts, or jade,
A Chinese mountain sculpture seen mid snow
Of Minnesota, or the soda bottle softened,
Sanded down along the Sound, beach glass that shone
Venetian in its luster, first arrival,
Gondoliers backlit at dawn upon
The green lagoon of history, behold
That glowing residue, four horses, Chios...

Span of moonscape, Trinitite results
From tests of Atom Bombs, the silica
And feldspar sucked up by a fireball
Into the rattling air, then melted, hailing
Like prophecy, & settling in sheets
Of sickly green (on second thought), that is
According to Professor Hermes, note.

We use gray water, flushed & scrubbed,
Brought back to us at bruising cost,
From mountains through the desert to the coast;
Impervious to infiltration, dwell
On asphalt islands, hardscape overheated,
Wavering as if the lot of what we saw,
That's everything, ourselves, were vapors.

Eclipse

The west of straitened ways, the towns of ghosts,
The Geiger counters, dosimeters,
Lithium deuterides… it ran away from them.

The Deuteronomist is sent to scan
Contaminants at Jackass Flats, reports
To base in confidence, to paraphrase:
I must read blasted Job. I'm none
Other than Death, World-Destroyer,
Terrible my feats of proof. The fire meshes,
Smashes nuclei. Now on we're sons
Of bitches. Here regard a sordid Church
Of Demiurge, a light that sears & beggars
Description, jealous, darkening all eyes.
Annihilation is within our hearts.
I know death now, its sacred thought."
We are too old & wise to stare into
That light directly, an eclipse.

Creative Ends

What euphemisms, Little Boy & Fat Man,
Glassy residue, the melting sky-blue lawn.
At Trinity, our hypocenter site,
Of lava rock, an obelisk, Osiris cry,
Amid a sea of glass a throne of doom,
Laved in the flood of thy bliss O Atom,
Swerves towards Golgotha: "These folks conceived
A lever, clever, moved the world over,
Wedded mind to instruments, but lacked
Creative ends..."

Coy, boyish jargon: Buster-Jangle,
Tumbler-Snapper, Upshot Knothole Grable;
Instruments tuned up to narrow down
The Margin of error in the practice of
Annihilation: Anvil, Sunbeam, Plumb Bob,
Latchkey, Touchstone, Crosstie, Teapot,
Flintlock, Nougat, Storax,
Phalanx, Bowline, Plowshare,
Quicksilver...

The Cat does play & after slay; as Xerxes
The Great did die, so too must you & I.
As runs the glass, man's life does pass.

Consoled Somehow

How could it have been different?
A boy, at Groton, Connecticut,
Along what once was called the Pequot River,
Connecticut, the arsenal of states,
My father friends with Captain So & So,
We took a tour aboard a submarine,
Atomic, capable of lasting months
Beneath the ocean, dark, without the need
Of surfacing, Persephone, death's seed.
It was the USS Kamehameha,
Decommissioned since. Immense,
Five stories high, it seemed quite cramped,
With thousands of instruments twangling…
Through the innards of this beast
Of prey we strolled, fierce beast
Of the apocalypse, at least
One variation on the theme,
Of catastrophic self-consuming feast…

I had a chance to lay
My warm palms on the tubes from which
They'd launch the warheads were
A strike command received & carried out.
The tubes were cold & hard.

Here hibernates a monster,
Ferocity potentially unleashed,
The cat as yet still in the bag,
A slash of lightning paws, at rest for now,

Behind a cool insouciance, except
To its predestined hunt, indifferent.
But thought of doom so close consoled somehow,
Dead instantly & not condemned to roam
Among the living where the bombs came down,
Who would remain & suffer,
Woman & child… through such a winter.

Will Range, Estranged

Can you recall a myth before this fact?
The cult of warriors confronts the cult
Of warriors. They saw away their limbs,
Reduced to torsos shovels toss into the air
When digging to construct another bank.
I weep, I grieve, I do not know I can
Not grieve & weep… provided I have looked.
The mother's yelling for her children, where
Shall I take you away from here, my angels?
If we die we die. The gods die too,
They said, with wisdom dreamed in sadness, lost
To history, their myths destroyed.
Don't despair: with each coming dawn
The dew's your lineage in residue.

What hell was raised in settling this dust.
Each must recall a noose averted, narrowly.
Orestes rests at last by hoist of God-
Machine: Athena throws a monkey wrench
Into the gears of cold revenge. This pioneer
Will range, estranged by history no more.
The others go on censoring themselves.
I cast away remorse upon prolonged
Arrival, passed, another test. But desert
Has reduced me to the elements,
One lonesome traveler, historical,
Beyond, from books to come, next Dust Bowl bard.
I burn within, a bigger light than most
Allow themselves, sing worried songs: it's hard.

Hearses, Rods

I'm armed with my annihilation to
The yellow of my teeth, anathema,
Anathema, from which I won't return, spent fuel,
Spent fuel, spent fuel, the empty bottles strewn
Like buds on hearses, rods & rods
Already spent, the cankered rose,
Remorse, another heavy change: Bring on
The smiling infant as the fog burns off.

Contemplate our death
The Roman way, a tragedy, the end
To Clio's story, asp, or Cato down
By moral certainty (green Hale hanged),
Petronius, his wrist let out with slits
In tragic gesture, languid, bloodless, dead,
A dutiful embrace of his own end.

Or opposite, an acrobat
Has fallen off the wire,
A butterfly
Beneath a crushing sole.

Life Is But

We've gathered, lost it all before: we had
To learn it wasn't ours to lose, just shared.
Freedom, mercy: we're dead already,
Totalized in futures dearly laid.
Can you recall our starting out, that shore?
I hear the rounds ejected, emptied shells.

I hear that dreary someone's day of doom:
This life is but a hill of difficulty,
Somnambulism epidemic, go
And stop signs most of it. I need to come
To terms with prejudicial schemes I use
To justify my trespasses, those murderous
Scenarios resulting from my pact
With my own peace, commence another life.
But all of this gave way to strife, I broke
My word, provoked catastrophe,
That giant mad as Aphrodite
(You will fade away & perish!) scorned.

Have Lowered

Before the splendors of the firmament
I now lament, take up mycology:
Lost travelers, unfit against this fall,
Some hide in caves on cliffs, their conscience free,
Some delve into the underground all night,
Some rashly plunge from bridges, leap from ships,
That drowning might expunge the devil's flame,
Some to the rocks & deserts stumble, cruise
The senseless blocks along the strips, for where
Is understanding? Vegas golden in the sun
Upon a sea of dusty glass, a voice
Resounds... you wonder, can this be the time?
What kingdom is at hand? We smell the lime.

The sun collapses like a keystone, fire-
Ant, humungous, gone into its mountain.
Feet & hands of man the conqueror
Have lowered, flattened, these & others for
Their latent energy to flower,
Roots of world trunk: we are
The apple bough & sunset limb, in hunt
For minerals, the good life underneath,
Eureka! Chop off all the tops
For jet black coal, molasses streams
Of slag left guzzling in ponds
Where nothing lives, so long as engines spark.

Empty Kingdoms

The vacancy is dark enough to see
The lactic nebulae, conceive black holes
And greyest anti-matter, drives, volitions,
Wills, the windy universe & us
Amid it, tinier than ever when
The city lights blocked out infinity,
Forcing us to squint an hour, more,
Before our eyes adjusted through this door
Into immensity, no end: we were
In awe from the beginning, saw anew
The sand we thought we knew so well, the soil
Made of diamonds, heard the ages sound
To wings that soar; estranging service guides,
Our tongues left tied amid the tumbling sage.

These holy ranges might start judging by
The flash & wash away our empty kingdoms
Jammed with mirror images, all ghosts
Too hurried, faces open, on from glory
To those bruises oozing out of Oz,
As through contaminated glass, unchanged,
We spot a range of possibilities,
In love with spontaneity. We symphonize
Our souls & mortify our enmity.
We look for crevices where bees & birds
Have hives & nests, the swallows hang
Their caves, embrace the scheme
Belief can acquiesce in, thrive,
Through course of grief, on lovers' gifts.

Won't Be Long

We contemplate another
Nowhere vigil, strange,
Hear skidding echoes, scuds,
Hissed brakes, those ghosts that plunge
Along on fumes,
Great tandem rigs
Whose engine nostrils snort,
Blow knots of phlegm, all pitchy
Petrol-breath, great thrashers,
Perching dragons, over
Silent prairies: speak of paradise
No more to me, these dragons
Guard the gates.

Into this world we're thrown, the song reminds,
We're frenzied as the vultures down
The road a mile, feasting in a wavy
Stew of flies, a carcass newly cast
Aside from which to draw a meaty bone,
Just slammed by chrome of hurling bumper,
Bloodstained dent the sole reminder
What remains is but a trace of it,
A butterfly
The windshield wipers swept away.

Halos abound down this sacrificial road,
Here a Mustang, there a Cougar,
Here a Thunderbird, & there an El Dorado...

All Meaningless Unless

The longest reign is Pluto's, split Plutonium.
I harp the pitchy depths & bend the beast
To hear the dauntless horn of Amphion
Wipe down the gleaming brass, amid great crowds
Bedimmed, that wake, like me, & crow: how came
I here? I've seen enough. The end is worse
Than any sign, all meaningless unless
I learn to see the bigger light. I drove
Six thousand days, saw sights invisible
And strange, a thirsty dove where nothing throve:
The tumbling sage might be the only thing
To move out there amid a corridor
Of shells, blue halls of dust, the mercury
In methyl form, invisible, what's sick
Arresting thoughts of slopes of green, the sand-
Traps multiplying, pummeling our hopes
For future smiles: see, shut your eyes
This desert says, inwrought with figures from
Dim coming times, unfathomable outer
Rim of eras, farthest scream from jammed
And dusty thoroughfares I fear no more:
I let their poison fill my ears & snore.
Please point me through this wilderness with just
A honey bag, a library, & smokes
To ease my hellish fall... Am I Ulysses
Grant, yet doomed to die of bleeding throat?
He burned it through with sour mash & rye,
The smoky oak to cut ignited sweet,
A ruminant who sucked & masticated vast,

Perpetual heaps of cigars, ten thousand down
In four long years of war, his lungs not un-
Like pitch, because to smoke them eased his war
Anxieties, checked pride, one of the nine
Out of ten Poor Richard said of men
Are suicides. Or Oppenheimer? Throat,
At 62. He saw that fabled fungus, huge,
Humungous, organs stressed within. Had one
Looked down from say, the moon, that dawn,
He would despise the omen: Humans asking,
Will you go with me to sudden doom?

Shell With Guts

A nudity of mud, this eve of Adam,
Ribbon, tomb be damned… A bomb that told
The spirits, rise: & so I wake to dream
A time before this cell, & recollect
The words of Herman Melville, who
To Nathaniel Hawthorne said
He'd made up his mind to be
Annihilated, north wind down
The dunes that night, the sand & shells
On the rattled shore, cigar in hand,
Chimney from his mouth.
He strung the tortoise shell with guts,
And now he chants how empty hell is,
While the world convulses & dissolves,
A song out of a shell along the shore.

Ceaseless Rolls, the Thrill

But in due time the megalopolis
Through milky smog emerged, as we crept down
The spine of interstate, a centipede,
Old West of railroads, the driven spike,
The lay of tracks, off circles almost circled,
Smoky diesel & bitumen thick
Enough to seal the roofs of Babylon,
To hang a garden in the desert.

Is it the law, amoral change?
A cog that's always greased for ceaseless rolls,
The thrill of which is not unlike the love
Two make, the roles of sand & sea
In harmony consumed, a constant plume imploring,
Panting heat, the waves delivering
This sound that heaves to set itself
And others free, a smashing rush & draw
Before it's through, away again, on high,
Those folds that seethe through lustiness to form,
That lash the poles of piers, crush sediment.
Can you remember, you, whose mother's face
Was beautiful, a time before this cell?
Sound depths: is this our lasting home?

Dissolve

A few revisit ancient chants for rain.
Socorro, Nuestra Señora del Socorro,
Lady of the Road, & you ahead,
Forgive me now, inheritance so grim,
So many eyes behind their weapons cold
And narrowed, no dance does except
To fertilize, console until ecstatic.
Strips of restaurants? Like links of chain.
Revert! Prophetic flickering: this sea
Of neon lunacy, of silica
Enflamed, a flowering the solar winds
Dissolve. We're hurling through larger worlds,
Tidal dust, magnetic stars. Can you
Recall a dream before these pounding shells?

This earth turns round the sun, but sun & earth
Are thrown at rates of speed we've dared
To contemplate, cut loose, away
From what, towards where, don't know,
Can't say, but love remains, amends
Near-tragedy, Atomic Lay, the best
To my capacity: may stem some grim
Well-armed unveiling of scars
To come. Orion's arm's our home,
One life, this local bubble, rim of fluff.

Section II

The Dandelion Clock

Blessed dandelion, stand for all creation,
Through your good we have this bowl to offer,
Leaves & flowers earth has given, human
Hands have cut & tossed with vinegar
And oil: it will become for us delightful food.
Bless the dandelion forever.

Brothers, sisters, pray that the dandelion's
Sacrificial death upon your lawns may be
Acceptable to God, whom you regard
As the almighty Maker, fathering us all.
May this God accept this salad bowl,
Which serves as evidence he is deserving
Of all our praise, for good food glorious
As this, the lion's tooth, the Piss in the Beds.

Lift up your heart to the light of the dawn
And see the dew is on the dandelions, bright
And beautiful, & wade through them, the sun
In every one of them a microcosm,
Come & see the dandelion, dewy in the dawn.

Holy Dandelion, lacking power, might,
Attacked by orthodoxy, blight
To those who wish for green unbroken, lawns
Of uniformity,
Heaven reflects in you the glory of earth,
O lowest midst the highest.
Blessed is he who sees in you the Lord:
O lowest midst the highest.

Let us proclaim the mystery of dawn,
The time of day the dandelion glows with dew,
Its golden petals pendulous with light.
Though dandelions die, new dandelions rise,
New dandelions come again. Dying they
Left uniformity, rising they
Brought back variety, Dandelion grow.
When we eat this salad, taste these leaves,
We eat the life that died to nourish us,
Proclaim it good for us, delightful diet,
Today & on until we dine no more,
Forever growing from the ground I love.
Deliver the dandelion from the blame
Commercials for the poisons claim
The weed deserves: they never wade at dawn
Through dewy lawns of it, don't know, don't want
To know the beauty there, disparaging
Its charms & claiming harms, they're paid to act
As if the dandelion is an anarchist,
It must be sacrificed,
The scapegoat ostracized.
O Dandelion, bend & bear the burden of
The sins of this world: mercy on us.

I know my dandelion lives, & last
Of all though it may be, I'll see it rise
Again at dawn, upon the dewy lawn
And wade up to my ankles through that gladness loose,
A glade as loud with gold as filled with bees,
Its meditations bottomless, its bean-
Rows dandelions, weeds to some, to me
Sublimity.

It took all day to clear the dandelions,
Till the whistle blew at three, the dice
Came out of pockets, soldiers drank their wine.
The emptiness the dandelions left
As yet remains unfilled, the lawns like glass
The squirrels also fleeing from the film

Of chemicals that lines the carpet's roots.
The children blew the dandelion clock
Apart & watched its parachutes disperse
Among the meadows left unmowed in fall.
You blow apart before the lips of youth
Your parachute-florets in petals
Aura round the usual
Culprit, nuisance, weed,
That dewy light at dawn, that lovely gold,
The crown of thorns
You are man's servant bent to suffer
Orthodoxy of Eradication.

Old tires, smell of them, the Astroturf
What looks like grass, glass, sand,
Petroleum dyed green, a nightmare
Version, demon, of the Grass a carpet,
Death, bitumen roofs of Babylon,
The artificial turf, the unofficial war
On dandelions, Christ
The dandelion war...

O Dandelion, gone,
You leave us white with fear & green with grave
Infection, breathless at the thought of death,
Our own, a perfect lawn grown over us.

Captain, USN

The old man, hair gone, from his recliner,
Radiation in his lungs, breathed
Last words into a tape machine, the room
Suffused with evening, the moon, I like
To think, alighting on his face, those eyes
So watery & red & full of love,
Right through the pane. He coughs & ashes, sniffs
The glass & clears his throat of clotting phlegm.

His wife was tall & elegant, her health
As yet intact, but always nervous, quiet,
Worried she would interrupt: his voice
Would stop, tape paused, till she apologized:
A ritual of love, to top his cup
When it ran dry, so he, a virtual
Soliloquist whose gestures I would never
Get to see, could press the button *play,*
Pour out his heart uninterruptedly.

Is it running? Am I being recorded?
I told your father, these cassettes must be
Preserved until you boys are old enough
To follow me along unflinchingly.
I hope my voice is still alive recorded;
I've lived through faults in all technology.
I want to speak to you about the farm,
And then the time I spent away at war.

Although the farm belongs to us no more,
Your blood is rooted to that land, those folks.

They did no harm, I like to think, although
In fact much harm was done along the way.
Like voices you provoke from open books,
They echo in my head, invoked for your
Sake, boys. Just make some time for listening,
And you'll find I am frank with you. It's all
The thanks I need to know you'll hear, & if
You do, then I'll be thanking you from out
Beyond the grave, where I've already gone
By now, as you consider this, if not yet now
For me: I know it could be any night.
Ohio roots, the ancient mounds, the farm:
So much of it remains to recollect,
Like bones on an abandoned battlefield,
Char & blur, fatalities obscure
The keenest eye, & well, this memory
Cannot be fixed; I lure the cat with winks
And sighs until she settles in my lap.
I'm kept awake by medicine or God
Knows what. Ohio stirs my mind.
Nobody's home is fixed, each path has forks,

My boots were soaked for years at sea, away,
But origins, somehow, still work in me
Some kind of magic spell responsible
For seeing things that came before I was,
The generations, four, three hundred acres
Farmed by folks I feel in me work.
Before this awful sickness came along
I had no time for mysticism though
Confronting death in battle woke in me
Some ancient sense of right & wrong. I am
Of scientific disposition when it comes
To wonders, though the verses I leafed through,
Memorized, even a boy, come back
To me like family. I must confess
Our ancestors remain in me: my mouth
Is raw like caves where heroes drew their names
On walls that flashed & warmed with living flames.

Those ancestors are using me to say
I know, I know, because they've seen it all,
Or I can see it all combining them,
Combined in me. I didn't want such thoughts
To fall upon deaf ears, so please do not
Dismiss this as an old man touched by madness
Or the medicine. It may be 3 AM,
Here comes another names for years unspoken,
Some, O hell! for forty years—I've fought
Off tears this way, by letting them be me
A while, letting me be them. It is
An act of love, my boys, you'll have to take
My word for it. My memory is not
A field crossed too often since the war
Came in between & kind of fenced it off,
And then your father's birth, life called, till now
That is, I'm dying. The point of view of doubt?
It edifies: from here I dote on it
Today, beyond ideas of faith, resigned
To love because I see in you the future,
All there is, a world made
Of correspondences & know
Compassion, joy, not just hard wars
And afterwards the scars, the harrowing,
The weary wary of too simplified
A tale, beneath, between the lines, they hide
A past from you that's useable, alive
If you can catch its speech, pronounce the words
You have inherited, but to the end
I can't foresee for you, enough to say
It's worth the work to keep a past that's yours,
And not just yours but that of other folks,
A common lot, your prime in fights abroad,
A boy at home you never get to see.
Much of the data's permanently lost,
Mere scraps, a palimpsest, such as
The ancient mummy wrappers, bits of text
Discarded mixed with paste, recalling flawed,

Unfinished thoughts, the mothball smell of trunks,
The randomness at times of what comes back
As vivid youth relived, in love again,
Adventuring, & what I can't retrieve,
Revenants that please to come & go.
I must consent to listen when the voice
Arrives. Memories you can't ignore
Will have their way with you, a brow
By worry furrowed, itch that can't be scratched
Beneath this withered, leather skin,
The vellum of this skull, & these weak arms
Mere flailing husks, once flexed with strength.
My eyes can't read for any length, the text
A scribbled mess of blurs. That's why I say
I hear you with my inner ear. The guns
I fired left me deaf enough. If you
Just let me play a bit you'll find it's not
A chore to listen in between the time
You dine & moments you begin to dream.

Listen, boys, death may be oblivion,
But stories have a way of living on,
So write things down on paper, they may keep,
Employ that leaky pen. Imagine, me
Waiting till near out of breath to turn on this
Machine & speak to you. If I had time,
And hadn't gotten sick, I would've noted
More of what I've learned; you'll earn a lot
To write about in living on the way,
Whatever comes, stay open to the wonder,
Boys, consumed as you may be...
You won't have to ransack your memory.
The USA will always go to war, boys,
The Second World War was fated mine.
I went to it with all the blessings known.
But why the constant war, the standing arms?
The myth comes manifest in news reports
No matter what the day or year it is.
The peace was always bracketed by strife.

Or put this way, the peace broke out sometimes
But not too often. Rotten news for life.
I think we'll never rest from war our way,
As one who takes his licks because, although
He doesn't like to be attacked, he knows
The rules of ceaseless war must dare
Such risks with some insouciance, & he
Defines the man he is by enemies
More often than he cherishes his friends.
The bruises he inflicts are meant to last.
You've read about the sordid wages, crimes
Against humanity, but Hemingway
Was on the mark, no war is not a crime.
I hate to say it but in time I've come
To see the wisdom in the adages
Of Mr. Franklin, bastard that he was:
All wars are follies, mischievous & costly.
"Infamy of servitude," I heard
It called somewhere, the silencing of men
Who have no wish to tear off Hector's shirt
Or shorten life already brief enough,
To swear along some stormy, war-torn shore
To sacrifice it all, like an Achilles.

We must strive patiently to solve disputes,
Enforce by arbitration, check the law...
Or else the ego's fountain cry of damage,
Fragmentary others, mounds of corpses,
Devil's harvest, names misspelled, unknown.

I say all this because I know by now
You're cognizant of how events march on.
You needn't take my word for evidence.
It's time you keep a record for yourself
So that the kids who follow you should know.
Whatever comes to mind, whatever keeps
You weeping, working, wanting to move on,
Enjoy a second look, consumed as you
May be, recall your family. I put

Away the most of it, but now I am
Contented, muse on luck I had: how though
I didn't have my own command, which hurt
Me at the time, I served great men, & now
Those Admirals are dying off, & so am I.
Just one of fewer left worth hearing now,
A veteran with something true to say
About this earth we knew when it was ours
To mar as we saw fit: some writers want
To know about it. Wouk for one. Pug Henry,
His novel's protagonist, is skipper of
Northampton when it sinks at *Guadalcanal.*
He sat, took notes with me on that, for scenes
Of battle, dialogue—it may be mine.
But all this talking, I'm worn out. I've got
To have a cigarette—which button's *Off?*

Hereaftermath

A caterwaul of dirty words, a spray
Of heated cries, unmusical,
The city's sucked into a weasel's hole.
A gutted sense of ruin, hard cold frost
Of bone incinerated, those who breathed
Up there, on high, the substance hanging
In heavy air, are particles to be
Picked up. It is a commonplace to find
A curl of hair, a ring, an acrid patch
Of silken blouse, a card, a melted purse,
The gaudiest cosmetics dashed against
The hungry, final ground, unmoved.
How strong the crush of gravity.
One must let go & throw oneself
Into a dirty world, cheapened as
The story falls into the fists of handlers,
Thugs & goons. The godlessness of it
Disgusts, to hear the deities invoked
In name, demonic, only, mired in
The tactics of the *Common Enemy*,
Malfeasor who bespatters any love
Not yet converted into hate. He weaves
A tapestry of threats, of boastful views.

He is a filthifying pyrolator with
A bone to pick, a sanctimonious
Applauder of brutality, a foil,
Typhon, bugbear, Fury, *fee-faw-fum*,
An ad man's sense of rhetoric,

In his attack convinced he's dust's
Ambassador, though from down here,
The intersection near, one sees
At base a babelizing pulpiteer,
Who'd fly into the face of any symbol's
Standing power, prove the frailty
Of more than skin, load-bearing skeleton,
The nerves of a society left frayed,
Folks crushed, their echoes ricocheting.
The priests are forced to utter "dust to dust"
Three thousand times, of ash & murder speak
With new authority. No matter whom
You have to thank, you catch a lasting theme
Amid the murdered jazz, this joyless zone:
"Perhaps it's just a dream, the germ of love
Out of the smack of violence, & lame
To speak collectively in such a case,
But I am moved by so much suffering,
Won't rattle these four walls to no effect.
Had I three hundred tongues, three thousand mouths …"
I am a citizen, don't just consume.

The littered streets reverberate with moans,
Most wanted postings, headlines hunt
For figures singled out to signify
The nihilistic tendency in man.
The glue of unction spills on everything.
Weep for the waste of souls that fell,
The crush of limbs, emotional
Unraveling, the words of final,
Whispered phrases, cough of fiberglass,
Asbestos, fireproofing: loss & failure
Come home. And thus the adversary
Has his function, goads the crowd in each:
Embraced by destiny of dust & ash,
Made up of shades, face winter shivering.
The crowd begins to realize the infinite,
Casehardened nature of equivalence,
Justified in hatred, tallies in its logs

Old ardency, a tale bound by fate,
A house still haunted for some past offense
Must burn. A voice declares "permanent
Emergency." The underhand looms large,
Grave secrecy, coercion. Infiltrate
By night, use methods of the flatfoot, dick,
To whom authority is might. Who's there?
He's tempted to abuse. Behind closed doors,
The house in white each day by midnight dons
Black cloaks, hates scrutiny. Those who for now
Inhabit it pontificate, myth-drunkards,
Doomed as mastodons, half-sunk in murk
That is the ammunition of their work.
Their show of power withers when they rest.

They must concede their signatures will be
Erased with every gust of change, no matter
What the range of their intelligence,
The irreducible result will be
The rawness of the wind-torn shore, sands stretched
Beyond the outposts of their vanity, their forts.

The Torturer, Insomnia, who will
Not be appeased, gawks down in paranoia
From her guarded tower, mind diseased.
Red eyes taxi, asphyxiating waves,
Take off for good. The forests of the world,
Merely wood, are piled on, a field
Cleared, a salt marsh filled for flight,
Religion spilt like lighter fluid, or
The noxious fumes from turbines, look,
Aloft: their rented vectors, moribund,
Their food although endangered not extinct.
They lift into the shattered sky above
Her steaming fill before eclipsed by drisk.
A hawk befalls half of a pair of doves.

Justice? What a quest. The court demands
A sacrifice: the witnesses won't testify,
Nor can you hear the evidence they will

Not cite. The lawyers banter back & forth
About *haruspical* procedures, poke
At life-less organs, make a case, as with
The ribs of birds when all the flesh is gone,
The final slivers underneath the cage.
They throw the bones into the tilting cups.
You hear the pundits in their screeds can't wait
To see a body on the scaffolding.
They blur the lines, the experts silent, lured
By spectacles so bloody fresh. Behold
The jury, baker's dozen from the local
Butcher's guild, the cosmic box of peers
Their shambles: smell the crematorium,
Hear the pitch of burning squeals, hogs
Of stinking pens adrift in heaps of garbage,
Range from courthouse dumpsters to the cans
Outside the greasy spoon next door. The smears
Stink up the stands & smash across the screens.
Catch drifting swine down on all fours to sniff
The aftermath, as if they'll spot some truffles.

All this despite the chase of dogs who live
To snap at heels, scratch an itch
They cannot reach, can't fetch or shed, no way
To purify, no way to get at it
Or shake it off, to cool what overheats
But wants to eat forever in the sun.
Now every penitent cries out for food,
Demands a sacrifice that yields but
A crumb upon the tongue, a plummeting
Of seedy husks into an empty well,
The walls of stone set echoing, hollowly,
Bottomless where soul was once assumed
To be, but long unfed, flames smother, grace
Forgotten, eating's over, not begun.

The soul? That bird has flown & left graffiti
Full of what it ate, digestion's siftings,
Wishbones shattered in a shifting tug of war.

Demanding Scavenger! How can I
Say anything if you don't say anything?
You mustn't be alarmed this filth does not
Wash off your face, from fruit already gone,
What's fresh cannot be eaten clean. The stain
Remains. Beware the many well-heeled pigs,
The nugatory pundits & their dogs:
They will be as they will, this pen of filth
Their private mine, each grill their office trough.
You cannot stand to let them get to you,
Another fate demands your discipline.

You want to live a sage, but cannot
Just defy the urge to rage
By gardening a private corner of
Our world, friend; this haunted field
Must be crossed before the end you keep
Imagining. Then when the time has come,
Though crowds demand the flow of blood,
The crowing mobs on buses, most abusive,
Give them all the lie, & plant
Your self up to your chin in mud:
Your vegetable love will grow. I've had
To flee the crowd, to butcher my own food,
I know, I swear, to really live—you'll find
Your buried roots restorative.

Down the Common Way

I

What can we know for sure? My guess is you,
Though half way home, have come to crave
The open road—& so do I. At dusk
Your exit doesn't take you far
Enough into the setting of the sun.
You often think, before you're done,
You'll follow where it bathes below the last
Horizon line, & long
For even further ones, where feelings blur,
Soul wild & loose, to rise as songs
Heard distantly—& so do I. But now,
Trunk crammed with work you must return tomorrow,
Deadlines mock your lack of liberty,
You can't escape the labor—nor can I.
What'll it solve to shake routine, let loose
For wider range, risk too much liberty?
Would that affright? We halt & creep, our focus
Getting there, dare not lose track: pain drags
On us. I will go farther, gradually,
You say, but fear you might seem mutinous.
The militant commute consumes reserves
Of energy you would have saved for love.
You're muttering, in sum, dim tales, vexed
Captivity, say freedom isn't as
It seems, mere tedium, refuses its
Responsibility, lacks sacrifice.
All freedom comes from laboring, fears, cares.
Retreats are childish & indefensible.

II

I cannot just fulfill my wish, deny
Its urgency, although I've been as one
Anemic craving iron, verging, drawn
To it magnetically, can't dodge the force
That drives through me at dawn, again at dusk.
In each of us a patient sick seeks far
Away for cures, imagines spas, is hot
To take a long, Quixotic tour. Between
Two lives, you question everything, & come
To wish for something more extreme,
The more the others hurry you each day,
The more the traffic causes you to pause,
A dream exotic, not this regiment
Of clutch & shift—I deem we're similar.
What is the joke—you'll call in well,
And take a break from work,
So that the vital,
Active voice in you can speak
Above the brawls, the pitch of quotes
Corrupting through the market's pit,
Perform a lustral rite.
Through crass
Aggression, gross
Demands, cruel waste,
We pass, two laughing souls
Out of the heart of soul-
Less trafficking,
Emerge unscathed.

III

I'll navigate, or drive, & we will pool
Our dream-power, strive to pass
Express through both the megalopolis
And soon its rural opposite, the road's
White arms embracing us, the moon
Embroidered with thin threads of cloud.
A part to wonder's spell, behold the whole
Sublime affair, a land of muddy blooms
It's tough to sniff, & difficult—
Amid aluminum & mercury—
For you, who would achieve a modicum
Of bravery, with soul to demonstrate,
Not to believe, as some, defeat's
Inevitable...
Nor dodge the ugliness, go right on through,
What holds deep worth for us has lurking force.
Regard the view with a removed delight,
Old pyramidal schemes, farfetched, steep grades.
Our ways austere, we slip past hucksters barking,
Slapping backs, shenanigans of marketing,
The glib but catchy little jingle fixed
To jangle in our psyches, needle over
Grooves in vinyl scratched—*obey this voice*
And cleave to it, since etched in us: we're mixed
Up with some item's brainless tune, a broad
Campaign, where few, you find, will call
By *beautiful* what you express to be;
They *beautify*—their sponsors fabulous.

IV

You can't avert your driven eyes, catch Argus
Gawking back at you; each intersection
Choked & bound forks off into infinity…
Beside myself, I wonder what I'd do
With wand in hand to wave off all of this,
Awaken folks or let them drift towards home.
Compassionate, we're finite in our patience,
Peacock-proud, depend on shorted fuel,
On forces seizing sources far from here
Brought close through wars our wheels fund,
Internalized combustion woes. All
Our contradictions packed into a car
A van or pick up truck, it's with a little
Bit of luck we brake for poetry.
We've wept & slept behind the wheel, served
Road food in vain, must vote such meals have
No love in them, consume the flaming booze;
Our voices engines, coughs, love's clear-
Well travelers, we talk in smoke. A wreck
Distracts, we stop the tape of *Moby Dick*,
Obliteration on the path, a mess
Of rubberneckers, fatal accident.
Such violence looms, such randomness evades
Our guard, though hard we'll try to ward away
Sure doom: the vehicles back up for miles,
Merge single file, ambulances hug
The shoulder, ruby sirens blaring there: too late
For them—frail souls provoke acute despair.

V

And yet into the thunder showers fresh
As flowers bursting forth we'd seize
Today to roam, unsponsored, ways we went
Not rivaling this freedom now: your soul's
Form bends with wonder wandering from dormancy
To wakefulness, aware, renewed, old rules
Unraveling. There's something out there
In us yet entwined, commensurate
With all we'll never solve, the moonlit paths
We'd otherwise leave snakes to rattle through,
The asphalt's monolith beneath us climbing
Mountains unimproved, a lunacy
Had we the quickest way in mind. We tack
And veer towards sympathy, revere the wind.
The spirit flips us rudderless towards soulfulness,
Uprooted sufferers, beyond the farce
Of surfaces, to songs heard distantly.
What's advertised won't last us through the test
Of solitude, it's not the stuff for ritual
Farewells. But sadness has its use: to sort
Out destinies, determine first things first,
Regain anew a single theme, & fling
Yourself into today, renew again
Your acumen: you'll win a renovated
View of life, as if the froth of sea
Foam washed it off, with each new tide a rod,
Faith-staff, knocked clean, divine caduceus.

VI

We'll risk more than an ankle's depth
To wade this surf, each revelation
Flashing, till we've lost the feet to move.
Forgive me that in you I see
Another wan & pale traveler
Whose gusto wanes. And yet the road
Lies plain before us, lengthened out, & ghost
Towns beckon us, the old deformities
Abandoned to the snakes, the burned out veins
Of mines. Divided Interstates will fade
As we turn off for courses free of them,
Until, before we must return, we will
Have reached the porch of blue obliteration,
Watched the beaches rattling with bones.
For all our love we'll know we're liminal.
Examine any conscience: first & last
The rule is rocks ground down to dust, the fire's
Love of growth, the blossoms dotting shafts
Of mines, if here or somewhere else, a song
Heard distantly. Remember when the grind
Resumes, our virtue palters, old regard
We hold for what's forgotten, overgrown,
The lore of windy paths, the silver mountains'
Azure zeniths, thrones of ghostly pines.
Each nameless spot of ground, the dented signs
All bleached by sun, each aftermath
Of rust & moth we come upon,
Might burst into a patch of mustard weed.

www.ingramcontent.com/pod-product-compliance
Lightning Source LLC
LaVergne TN
LVHW041550070426
835507LV00011B/1025
* 9 7 8 1 9 0 9 8 4 9 3 5 8 *